# SITH WARS

LONDON, NEW YORK, MUNICH,
MELBOURNE AND DELHI

**Editors** Lisa Stock, Julia March, Pamela Afram,
Hannah Dolan, Garima Sharma
**Senior Editor** Victoria Taylor
**Senior Designer** Lisa Sodeau
**Designers** Owen Bennett, Richard Horsford,
Toby Truphet, Chitrak Srivastava,
**Pre-Production Producer** Marc Staples
**Producer** Danielle Smith
**Managing Editor** Laura Gilbert
**Design Manager** Maxine Pedliham
**Publishing Manager** Julie Ferris
**Art Director** Ron Stobbart
**Publishing Director** Simon Beecroft

**Reading Consultant** Linda B. Gambrell, PhD.

**For Lucasfilm**
**Executive Editor** Jonathan W. Rinzler
**Art Director** Troy Alders
**Keeper of the Holocron** Leland Chee
**Director of Publishing** Carol Roeder

First American Edition, 2014
13 14 15 16 10 9 8 7 6 5 4 3 2 1
Published in the United States by DK Publishing
345 Hudson Street, New York, New York 10014

Published in Great Britain by Dorling Kindersley Limited.

A catalog record for this book is available from the Library of Congress.

DK books are available at special discounts when purchased in bulk for
sales promotions, premiums, fund-raising, or educational use.
For details, contact:
DK Publishing Special Markets
345 Hudson Street
New York, New York 10014
SpecialSales@dk.com

ISBN: 978-1-4654-1814-2 (Hardback)
ISBN: 978-1-4654-1725-1 (Paperback)

Color reproduction by Alta Image
Printed and bound in China by South China

Discover more at
**www.dk.com**
**www.starwars.com**

# Contents

# TIMELINE OF
# THE SITH

This timeline shows the main events in the galaxy that have affected the Sith. Time is ordered around a legendary conflict called the Battle of Yavin.

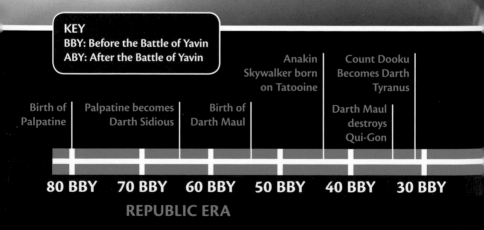

**KEY**
**BBY: Before the Battle of Yavin**
**ABY: After the Battle of Yavin**

Anakin
Skywalker born
on Tatooine

Count Dooku
Becomes Darth
Tyranus

Birth of
Palpatine

Palpatine becomes
Darth Sidious

Birth of
Darth Maul

Darth Maul
destroys
Qui-Gon

80 BBY    70 BBY    60 BBY    50 BBY    40 BBY    30 BBY

REPUBLIC ERA

Anakin becomes
Darth Vader

Luke Skywalker
duels Darth Vader

Darth Vader destroys
Darth Sidious

**20 BBY**   **10 BBY**   **0**   **10 ABY**   **20 ABY**   **30 ABY**

EMPIRE ERA            **NEW REPUBLIC ERA**

# Reign of Evil

A long time ago, the galaxy was ruled by an evil Sith Lord named Darth Sidious. He was also known as Emperor Palpatine. He used fear and corruption to rule his evil Empire.

The Sith is an ancient order that uses the dark side of a mysterious energy called the Force to fuel their terrible powers. The Force is created by all living creatures, but it can be controlled only by a few special people. There is also a light side of the Force, which is used for good.

In these pages you will meet the evil Sith who started many wars, aiming to terrify the galaxy and divide its people. You will also meet many evildoers who were allied with Darth Sidious and the Sith. Finally you will meet the brave few who dared to stand up against Darth Sidious and the Sith, and often faced tragic consequences for their bravery.

# Jedi and Sith

The Sith Order was formed
thousands of years ago when a
member of another order, called
the Jedi, turned to the dark side of the Force.
Others followed him and became Sith, too.

The Jedi are very different from the Sith.
They, too, are experts in using the Force,
but they are not interested in power for
themselves. Instead, they seek justice for
all, and use the light side of the Force to
maintain peace and order in the galaxy.
Their opposing beliefs have made Jedi
warriors the main enemy of the Sith.

The Sith believe that the dark side of
the Force is more powerful than the light.
Turning to the dark side can bring great
power quickly, while the Jedi have to study
the light side of the Force patiently for
many years before they are able to master it.

The Jedi believed that they had destroyed
all the Sith a thousand years ago. In fact,
one Sith survived and went into hiding,
determined to return stronger than before
and wreak revenge on the Jedi.

# THE
# SITH CODE

The Sith Code is a mantra that demonstrates the Sith Order's core beliefs. Its chilling words explain why the dark side of the Force is surrounded by so much fear and mystery.

Peace is a lie,
there is only passion.
Through passion,
I gain strength.
Through strength,
I gain power.
Through power,
I gain victory.
Through victory,
my chains are broken.
The Force shall free me.

# The Rule of Two

Thousands of years ago, there were many Sith.

Their allegiance to the dark side, however, made them greedy and selfish. Each Sith was concerned only with his own interests and so they often disagreed with each other, fighting to the death. As a result, the Sith nearly destroyed themselves.

The Rule of Two was introduced to save the Sith Order. This rule states that there can be only one Sith Master and one apprentice at any time. It accepts that Sith will always try to destroy each other and ensures there will always be one surviving Sith.

When the apprentice becomes more powerful than the Master, he destroys his Master and chooses an apprentice of his own. There can be no loyalty among the Sith, only fear and suspicion.

> *"Two there should be. No more, no less.
> One to embody power, the other to crave it."*

**ANCIENT SITH LORD**

# Sith Powers

The Sith have some truly terrifying powers. To use them, they must draw energy from the dark side. They encourage destructive emotions like anger and hatred within themselves in order to boost their dark side powers.

The Sith use the Force to control people's minds and are merciless in battle. They can also use their dark side energies to throw heavy objects, crushing their enemies.

The dark side of the Force gives the Sith powers that even the Jedi do not have, but these can be unpredictable. One of these powers is deadly Force lightning, where the Sith channel the Force through their bodies to fire bolts of energy from their fingers at opponents. These lethal charges cause intense pain and weaken the victim. It is a challenge for even the most powerful Jedi Master to deflect such bursts.

If a Jedi does successfully deflect them, however, the consequences can be disastrous for the Sith. A Jedi Master named Mace Windu did just that when Darth Sidious attacked him with Force lightning. The lightning hit Sidious's face and scarred him forever.

# Force Weapon

The Sith and the Jedi may be opposing orders who use the Force in very different ways, but they do share a common weapon—the lightsaber.

The Sith and the Jedi are the only people in the galaxy who use the lightsaber. It is the ancient weapon of the Jedi Order, but since the Sith descended from the Jedi, they use them, too.

The lightsaber is a sword that contains a special energy crystal in the heart of its handle. The crystal creates a brightly colored blade of pure energy that can cut through almost anything. Sith lightsaber blades are usually red and are made from artificial crystals, while the blades of Jedi lightsabers are blue, green, or occasionally purple, and are made from natural crystals. Each Sith or Jedi builds their own lightsaber, so each one may suit the owner's individual personality and fighting style.

The Sith do, in fact, have enough Force power to battle without a lightsaber, but each Sith apprentice learns to use one as part of their training.

# DARK POWERS

Members of the Sith Order use many deadly and dangerous powers. Each power is channeled through a different part of the body and can produce devastating results.

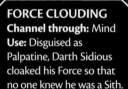

**FORCE CLOUDING**
**Channel through:** Mind
**Use:** Disguised as Palpatine, Darth Sidious cloaked his Force so that no one knew he was a Sith.

**FORCE CHOKE**
**Channel through:** Hands
**Use:** A Sith Lord can use the Force to choke people without even touching them.

**FORCE LIGHTNING**
**Channel through:** Hands
**Use:** Darth Sidious often used the deadly Force lightning on his enemies.

## POWER OVER DEATH
**Channel through:** Body and mind
**Use:** Sidious used the Force to save a Sith Lord's life.

## TELEKINESIS
**Channel through:** Hands
**Use:** The Sith can move heavy objects without actually lifting them.

## TEMPTATION
**Channel through:** Mind
**Expert:** Darth Sidious claimed to have the tempting power of immortality.

## MIND CONTROL
**Channel through:** Mind
**Use:** A Sith Lord can use the Force to control minds, but a strong Jedi can resist it.

# Senator Palpatine

After the Jedi thought they had destroyed the Sith, the galaxy became a Republic. It was ruled peacefully by the Senate—a group of elected representatives from each planet. The representative for the planet of Naboo, Senator Palpatine, was very popular. He impressed many people with his decisive approach to politics and was liked and trusted by all. But underneath his friendly exterior he was hiding a very dark secret: He was actually the evil Sith Lord Darth Sidious and was waiting to launch a sinister plot to take over the galaxy!

Darth Sidious was secretly behind an invasion of the peaceful planet of Naboo by an evil business organization. When Naboo's Queen Amidala asked the Senate to help her to defend her planet, Senator Palpatine was very eager to assist her. His efforts to bring about peace seemed to end in great success.

The Senate and the Jedi were impressed, especially when Palpatine promised to end corruption in the galaxy, too. Confident that the Senate supported and trusted him, Darth Sidious knew he could put the next stage of his secret plan into action without detection.

# Evil Genius

Darth Sidious was one of the most powerful Sith who has ever lived. He craved supreme power so that he could force every planet to do what he wanted. To achieve this, Darth Sidious needed a dual identity.

Sidious disguised himself as the peaceful Senator in order to trick his Jedi enemies, destroy the Senate, and seize control of the galaxy. Sidious's powers of deception were so strong that he was able to conceal from

everyone the fact that Senator Palpatine was actually a Sith Lord in disguise.

Almost no one knew that Darth Sidious existed, let alone what he looked like. Even when speaking to his evil allies, Sidious always wore a hooded black cloak to conceal his face. He also gave orders via hologram so that he never revealed his exact location.

In accordance with the Rule of Two, Sidious became a Sith Master by murdering his own Master, Darth Plagueis. He took an apprentice, Darth Maul, to help carry out his evil plans.

# Phantom Menace

For a thousand years, the galaxy was united in peace as a democracy. This meant that every person in all of the different planets of the Republic had the chance to be heard, and large armies were outlawed. All laws were passed in the Senate building, a gigantic, circular construction on the galaxy's capital planet, Coruscant.

After tricking the Senate into thinking that he had brought about peace on Naboo, Palpatine convinced the senators to make him the Supreme Chancellor. This gave him the power to make all the decisions in the Republic.

Later, Sidious crowned himself Emperor and the Sith Lord ruled the entire galaxy. Emperor Palpatine began at once to build a massive army, intent on destroying the Jedi Order once and for all. It seemed as though no one could stop him.

# OFFICE OF THE
# CHANCELLOR

Chancellor Palpatine's office may have looked like a typical Senator's office from the outside, but there were clues to his real identity all around.

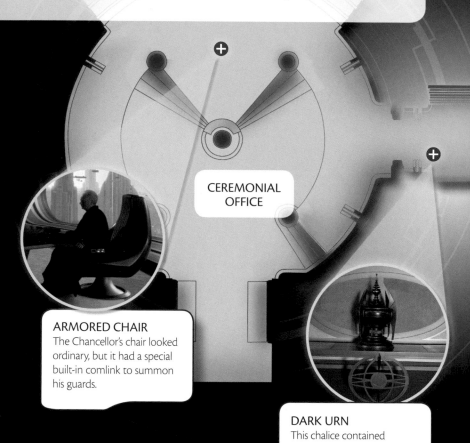

CEREMONIAL
OFFICE

**ARMORED CHAIR**
The Chancellor's chair looked ordinary, but it had a special built-in comlink to summon his guards.

**DARK URN**
This chalice contained Korribanian incense for conducting a Sith Fire Ritual.

## RELICS OF THE SITH
The two ornate black vases were Spirit Urns, which held the remains of former Sith Lords. The vases were placed at the entrance of Palpatine's Private Office.

## PRIVATE OFFICE
Palpatine used the computers in his secure private office to secretly communicate with his Sith apprentice. This was also where he stored his plans to take over the galaxy.

PRIVATE
OFFICE

## DECEPTIVE ART
The artwork on the wall slyly glorified the Sith at war with the Jedi.

## HIDDEN WEAPON
This statue showed an ancient philosopher of the dark side. It also concealed Palpatine's lightsaber.

# SENATOR
# AND SITH

The evil strength of the dark side of the Force ravaged Darth Sidious's entire body. The effect was most apparent on the Sith Lord's face: His wrinkles deepened and his complexion grew paler. Simultaneously, his alter ego, Palpatine, also began to show the strain.

**SENATOR PALPATINE**

**SUPREME CHANCELLOR**

## Using the Force
Channeling the dark side of the Force can have an instant effect on the appearance of its user. When Sidious created an intense burst of Force lightning, his body weakened and the color drained from his face.

DARTH SIDIOUS      EMPEROR PALPATINE

# The Jedi

Only the Jedi have the powers to face the evil Sith.

Learning to be a Jedi and to use the light side of the Force takes many years of intense training. Those who become Jedi begin their training as children. They learn lightsaber skills and the ability to remain calm in all situations. Later, they may be chosen by experienced Jedi Masters to become their Padawans.

The Jedi use the Force to keep peace in the galaxy, which means that they must stop those who use the dark side to do evil. The Jedi can actually listen to the Force telling them that there is trouble happening somewhere. This is

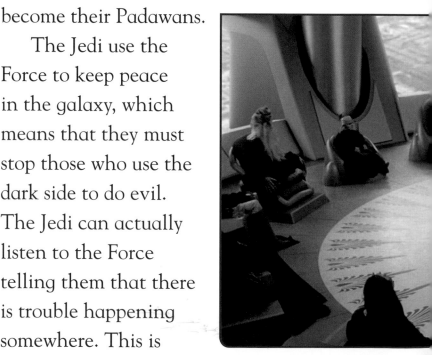

known as a disturbance in the Force. Once the Jedi feel it, they have to find the source and do all that they can to solve the problem.

The Jedi are guided by twelve of the wisest and most experienced Jedi, who are known as the High Council. They include Grand Master Yoda, Mace Windu, and Ki-Adi Mundi. All decisions about who should become a Jedi and how the Jedi must act are made by the members of the Council.

# WHO TRAINED
# WHOM?

Each Padawan or Sith apprentice receives training from a Master skilled in the Force. Their lessons are passed down the generations, from Master to apprentice.

### YODA
Yoda was the oldest and most powerful Jedi in the order. He has trained many young Jedi over the years.

### COUNT DOOKU
Although he was trained by Yoda, Dooku expressed controversial ideas about the Jedi Order.

### QUI-GON JINN
Count Dooku's Padawan was often outspoken and rebellious, but he was always loyal to the Jedi Order.

**THE JEDI**

### DARTH SIDIOUS
The most evil of all Sith Lords, Darth Sidious took on a series of apprentices, training them to embrace the dark side.

### DARTH MAUL
From a young age, Darth Maul was trained as Sidious's apprentice in secret.

**THE SITH**

## KI-ADI-MUNDI
This Master began his training at a late age, but Yoda helped him to become a skilled Jedi.

## LUKE SKYWALKER
Yoda's final student was Luke Skywalker. Yoda trained Luke in the ways of the Force so he could fulfil his potential and save the galaxy.

## OBI-WAN KENOBI
As a Padawan, Obi-Wan struggled with his rash temperament. Qui-Gon's training helped him become a model Jedi.

## ANAKIN SKYWALKER
Obi-Wan developed a strong bond with Anakin. Obi-Wan believed his Padawan was gifted, but impatient.

## DARTH TYRANUS
Count Dooku was tempted to the dark side with promises of great power. He became Darth Tyranus.

## DARTH VADER
After losing faith in the Jedi, Anakin became Darth Sidious's final apprentice, Darth Vader.

# Darth Vader

Darth Vader was one of the most deadly Sith apprentices ever. He ruled the galaxy with his Master, Darth Sidious. Vader's knowledge of the dark side of the Force made him a powerful and dangerous figure.

Vader was merciless in battle and would kill anyone who got in his way or disobeyed him. He used a Force choke to strangle people without even touching them, and wielded many other terrifying Force powers.

Darth Vader always wore a black suit of protective armor and a hard black mask. This armor was created in a secret medical facility because his body had been almost destroyed in a great battle. His armor and mask contained breathing equipment and life-support systems to keep him alive.

The only place where Vader could safely remove his helmet was in a special isolation chamber, where mechanical arms lifted the helmet from his scarred head.

The wheezing sound made by Vader's breathing apparatus was enough to strike terror in the mind of anyone he approached.

# DARTH VADER'S
# ARMOR

Darth Vader's armor was protective in battle, and the highly complex suit he wore also had many different systems for keeping him alive.

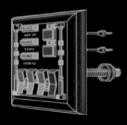

**LIFE-SYSTEMS COMPUTER**
The chestplate controlled Vader's life-support system. Switches allowed him to change the functions that kept him alive.

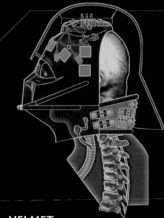

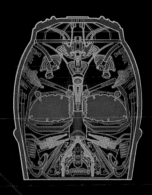

## SENSORY ENHANCERS

Goggles filtered out light that might cause further damage to Vader's eyes.

## HELMET

Darth Vader's helmet helped him to breathe. It cycled oxygen in and out of his broken lungs.

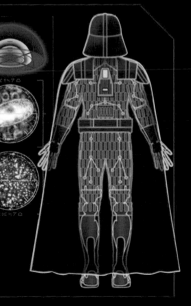

## LIFE SUPPORT SYSTEMS

Vader's suit was lined with monitors that checked his heart, brain, blood, and nerve activity and helped to keep him alive.

# Anakin Skywalker

Before he became a Sith Lord, Darth Vader was a Jedi named Anakin Skywalker. Anakin was one of the most talented Jedi ever. His Force powers were incredibly strong, but Anakin was impatient. He wanted to become more powerful than any other Jedi.

Anakin did not agree with some of the Jedi rules. He secretly married Senator Padmé Amidala, even though Jedi are forbidden to marry.

Darth Sidious noticed Anakin's discontent. He felt he could lure him to the dark side and make him his Sith apprentice. As Palpatine, Sidious gained Anakin's trust and began to convince him that the dark side of the Force was more powerful than the light side. He also told Anakin that he could stop Padmé from dying. When he heard this, Anakin rejected his Jedi training and joined Darth Sidious. But Sidious was wrong. Only years later would Anakin discover that Padmé had given birth to babies before she died.

As a Sith, Anakin killed many Jedi. He even fought his former best friend, Obi-Wan Kenobi. They battled on the edge of a lava river until Obi-Wan managed to strike Anakin down. Anakin fell near the lava and was burned nearly to death. Darth Sidious rescued him, and rebuilt his body with robotic parts and an armored suit. Darth Vader was born!

*"I'm not the Jedi I should be. I want more—but I know I shouldn't."*

**ANAKIN SKYWALKER**

*"The boy is dangerous."*

**OBI-WAN KENOBI**

*"Twisted by the dark side, young Skywalker has become."*

**YODA**

*"I don't trust him."*

**MACE WINDU**

*"The Force is strong with you! A powerful Sith you will become."*

**DARTH SIDIOUS**

# PATH TO THE
# DARK SIDE

Anakin Skywalker possessed many fine qualities
that made him a great Jedi. But his constant struggle
to control his feelings made him vulnerable to the
dark side of the Force.

**DEDICATION**
Anakin was
impatient at
times, but he
proved to be a
loyal Padawan
to Obi-Wan.

**POTENTIAL**
As a child, Anakin
showed great skill,
but also fear. The Jedi
were unsure about
training him.

**ANGER**
When Anakin's
mother died at the
hands of Tusken
Raiders on Tatooine,
Anakin gave in to his
anger and destroyed
the whole clan.

**DEFIANCE**
Anakin broke Jedi
rules and married
Padmé Amidala in
secret. His fear of
losing Padmé made
him blind to all else.

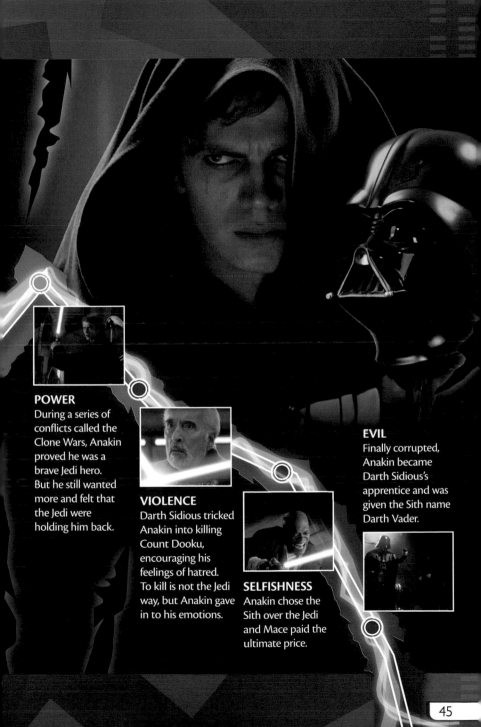

## POWER
During a series of conflicts called the Clone Wars, Anakin proved he was a brave Jedi hero. But he still wanted more and felt that the Jedi were holding him back.

## VIOLENCE
Darth Sidious tricked Anakin into killing Count Dooku, encouraging his feelings of hatred. To kill is not the Jedi way, but Anakin gave in to his emotions.

## SELFISHNESS
Anakin chose the Sith over the Jedi and Mace paid the ultimate price.

## EVIL
Finally corrupted, Anakin became Darth Sidious's apprentice and was given the Sith name Darth Vader.

# Darth Maul

Long before Vader, Darth Sidious's first apprentice was a savage alien from the planet Dathomir named Darth Maul. Darth Sidious discovered Maul's Force-potential when he was an infant. He immediately began raising Maul with the intention of making Maul his apprentice someday.

Sidious's training methods were often harsh and unforgiving, but as a result Darth Maul became a strong and relentless fighter. He harnessed powerful emotions, such as anger and hatred, to gain strength from the dark side. He fought using a double-ended lightsaber, also called a saberstaff.

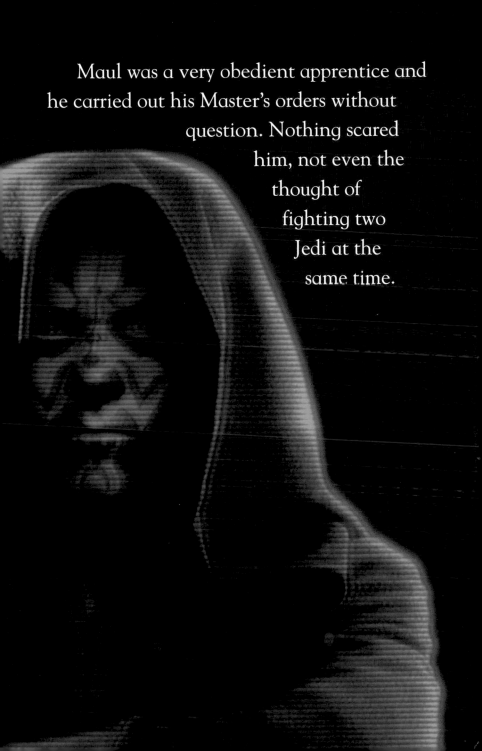

Maul was a very obedient apprentice and
he carried out his Master's orders without
question. Nothing scared
him, not even the
thought of
fighting two
Jedi at the
same time.

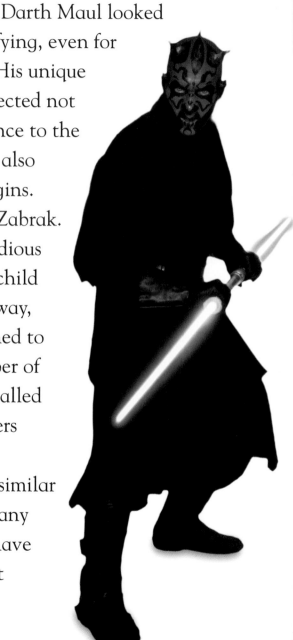

# Zabrak Warrior

Darth Maul looked terrifying, even for a Sith. His unique appearance reflected not only his allegiance to the dark side, but it also revealed his origins.

Maul was a Zabrak. Before Darth Sidious found him as a child and took him away, Maul was destined to become a member of a warrior tribe called the Nightbrothers of Dathomir.

Zabraks are similar to humans in many ways, but they have a few significant differences.

This species can have many colored skin tones, including red, yellow, brown, and black. Zabraks have horns on their heads, which appear early in life and can grow in varying numbers and patterns on their heads. They also display distinctive and detailed facial tattoos. These tattoos symbolize family loyalty and place of birth, or can reflect the personality of the individual Zabrak. Maul's face was tattooed with dark side symbols and he had yellow eyes—another physical sign that he was a powerful Sith devoted to the dark side of the Force.

Maul's Force powers were strong, but even this deadly Sith needed special equipment and vehicles, like a speeder bike, to help him track down the Jedi.

# SPEEDERS AND STARSHIPS

The Sith have developed many vehicles to serve a variety of sinister purposes. Each Sith selects his vehicle depending on his mission.

Command tower

Solar arrays

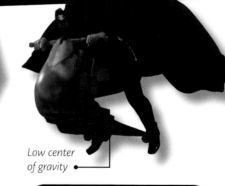

Laser cannon

Low center of gravity

## TIE ADVANCED X1
PILOT: Darth Vader
SIZE: 9.2 m (30 ft) long
MAX. ACCELERATION: 4,150 G
CAPACITY: 1 pilot
WEAPONS: 2 laser cannons

## GEONOSIAN SPEEDER
PILOT: Darth Tyranus
SIZE: 3.2 m (10 ft 7 in) long
SPEED: 634 km/h (394 mph)
CAPACITY: 1 pilot
WEAPONS: None

## SUPER STAR DESTROYER, EXECUTOR

SIZE: 19,000 m (62,336 ft) long
MAX. ACCELERATION: 1,230 G
CAPACITY: 280,735 crew, 38,000 passengers
WEAPONS: 5,000 turbolaser and ion
cannons, 250 concussion missile batteries,
40 tractor beam projectors

*Turbolaser computer targeting*

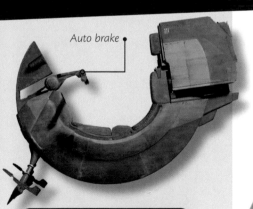

*Auto brake*

*Laser cannon*

*Cockpit*

## SITH SPEEDER, BLOODFIN

PILOT: Darth Maul
SIZE: 1.65 m (5 ft 6 in) long
SPEED: 650 km/h (404 mph)
CAPACITY: 1 pilot
WEAPONS: None

## IMPERIAL SHUTTLE

PILOT: Darth Sidious
SIZE: 20 m (66 ft) long
MAX. ACCELERATION: 1,400 G
CAPACITY: 6 crew, 20 passengers
WEAPONS: 2 twin laser cannons,
1 twin blaster cannon

# Dark Plan

Darth Sidious was
determined to wait until just
the right moment to unleash his
apprentice Darth Maul on the Jedi. He was
convinced that no Jedi would be a match
for a deadly Sith like him!

Jedi Qui-Gon Jinn and Obi-Wan Kenobi
had landed their damaged starship on the
desert planet Tatooine, where they were
looking for repairs. The Sith located the
starship and knew that the Jedi must be near.

Maul was tasked with discovering the exact location of his enemies, and he sent three probe droids to gather this information.

The tiny Dark Eye droids were controlled by Maul's wrist link and were perfectly suited to tracking on a planet's surface, rather than in space. They contained image sensors that could send important data back to Maul and were designed to pass through crowds silently and largely unnoticed. One of the droids located Qui-Gon Jinn. The Sith was ready to begin his deadly mission.

**A LETHAL TASK**
On Tatooine, Darth Maul approached the place where Qui-Gon Jinn had been located, looking out for his target.

# Sith Attack!

The moment that Darth Maul had been training for had come at last. He was about to test his skills in a battle against the Sith's greatest enemy—the Jedi.

While waiting for his ship to be repaired, Jedi Master Qui-Gon Jinn sensed a disturbance in the Force. Something was wrong, but what? Suddenly, a cloaked figure appeared in the distance on a speeder bike.

When Darth Maul attacked, it came as a double shock to Qui-Gon. Not only was the attack unexpected, but his opponent was wielding a lightsaber and using skills similar to his own. Jedi and Sith did battle until Obi-Wan arrived with the repaired starship. Qui-Gon managed to use a Force jump to board the ship and escape. The battle was over—for now. The Jedi knew that this attack meant only one thing: The Sith were back.

# Jedi Ways

Despite their Force powers, the Jedi could not foresee the return of the Sith. They needed to summon all their strength and work together to face the threat of the dark side. Fortunately, Jedi are good at working together.

The Jedi do not follow the Rule of Two—there can be as many Jedi as can prove themselves worthy of the name. Indeed there is no limit to the number of Jedi in the Jedi Order. A Master can train more than one apprentice at the same time.

Like the Sith, the Jedi practice a Master and apprentice system. However, a Jedi Master acts very differently from a Sith Master! A Jedi Master trains his apprentice or Padawan with patience. He passes on his own skills and hopes that one day his Padawan will become a Jedi Knight and then a Jedi Master. The Master and Padawan relationship is based on loyalty and respect, not fear.

Qui-Gon Jinn was a wise and experienced Jedi Master. He had great hopes for his Padawan Obi-Wan Kenobi, who displayed formidable lightsaber skills, and the two Jedi developed a very close bond.

# QUI-GON JINN

Qui-Gon believed in the Jedi way, but he had a rebellious streak and he was quick to speak his mind.

## DATA FILE

**Species**: Human
**Rank**: Jedi Master
**Birthdate**: 92 BBY
**Trained by**:
Count Dooku
**Combat style**:
Form IV (Ataru)
**Trademark**:
Independent thinking

**Risk-taker**
When Qui-Gon found Anakin on Tatooine, he noticed something special in the slave boy. He risked losing his ship in a bet to win Anakin's freedom.

# OBI-WAN KENOBI

Obi-Wan was a model Jedi. He was humble and steadfast, but he could be combative if necessary.

**Focused**
Obi-Wan was known for his ability to keep calm under pressure. This quality made him a fearsome opponent in space battles.

## DATA FILE
**Species**: Human
**Rank**: Jedi Master
**Birthdate**: 57 BBY
**Trained by**:
Qui-Gon Jinn
**Combat style**:
Form IV (Ataru); later,
Form III (Soresu)
**Trademark**: Skilled
negotiation

# Deadly Lightsaber

Every Sith and every Jedi builds their own lightsaber. Consequently each one matches the personality and fighting style of its owner.

Darth Maul found that a regular single-bladed lightsaber was not powerful enough for him. Instead he created a unique double-bladed weapon known as a saberstaff by welding two separate lightsabers together. Its design was based on an ancient Zabrak weapon called a Zhaboka.

The twin blades made the saberstaff twice as deadly as the single-bladed lightsabers used by the Jedi. This also meant that Maul could take on two opponents at once.

The saberstaff was twice the size of a lightsaber. It took Maul many years of training before he was agile and athletic enough to wield it effectively in combat.

On his first mission for Darth Sidious, Maul proved himself with his weapon against the Jedi Qui-Gon Jinn.

# SITH
# LIGHTSABERS

Sith lightsabers are recognized by their sinister red glow. They are powered by synthetic red crystals, which reflect the Sith's rage.

## DARTH
## TYRANUS

On becoming a Sith, Count Dooku traded his green Jedi blade for a red one.

## DARTH
## MAUL

Darth Maul's saberstaff could be split into two separate lightsabers.

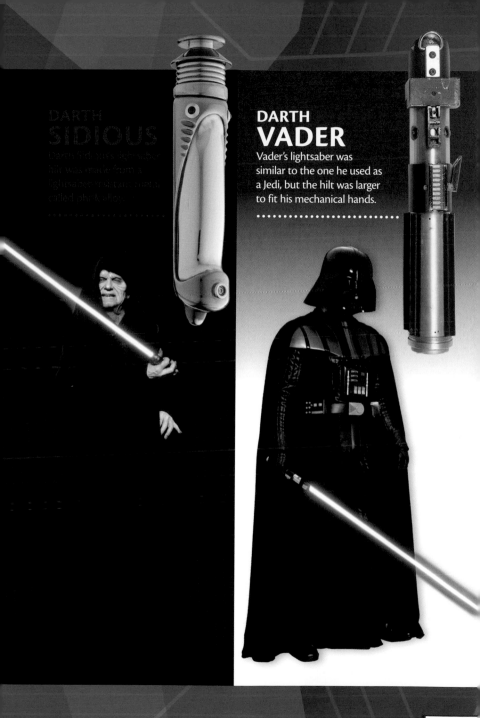

Darth Sidious's lightsaber
hilt was made from a
lightsaber-resistant metal
called phrik alloy.

## DARTH
## VADER

Vader's lightsaber was
similar to the one he used as
a Jedi, but the hilt was larger
to fit his mechanical hands.

# Sith Combat

The unique double-sided nature of Darth Maul's saberstaff led the Sith apprentice to develop his own form of lightsaber combat. The Sith warrior used elements from a lightsaber combat form called Juyo. This form allowed him to take advantage of his natural athletic abilities and agility in battle, using martial arts moves to add an element of surprise. He also studied a style of fighting called Niman,

which focused on balance, specifically designed for combat with dual blades.

Maul drew on his dark side emotions to increase his power in battle. During a duel, the Sith entered a trance-like state, so that he could focus entirely on his saberstaff.

But Darth Maul did not rely on his lightsaber skills alone to win a fight. The Sith also planned an attack very carefully.

When he fought Qui-Gon Jinn and Obi-Wan Kenobi on Naboo, Darth Maul tactically separated the two Jedi so that he could destroy them one at a time. He battled the skilled Jedi Master Qui-Gon first. The Sith Lord proved to be a superior fighter and he dealt the Jedi a fatal blow.

# The End of Maul

Darth Maul's passion and rage made him a fearsome opponent. Obi-Wan Kenobi tried to use his grief at the loss of his Master, Qui-Gon Jinn, to fuel his own attack against the Sith. However, it is not the Jedi way to act on emotions or to seek revenge. This causes the Jedi to lose their focus, which can have fatal consequences in battle.

Obi-Wan's anger led him to lose his cool as he launched a vicious assault against Darth Maul. The Sith took advantage of Obi-Wan's unfocused rage, using the Force push to throw him over an abyss. The Sith believed he had finally achieved his goal of destroying the Jedi. But Maul underestimated his opponent. Obi-Wan remembered his training and regained his calm, summoning all his strength to jump up high and grab his Master's lightsaber. With one deadly blow Obi-Wan defeated an unsuspecting Darth Maul.

# SITH
# ARTIFACTS

Many of these items are used by the Sith to help them on evil missions. Some are ancient objects, which the Sith especially treasure as they reflect the long history of the order.

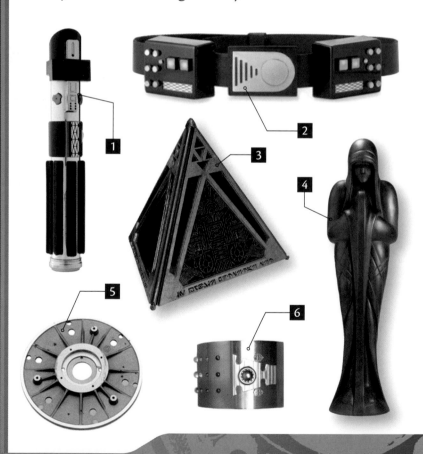

1

2

3

4

5

6

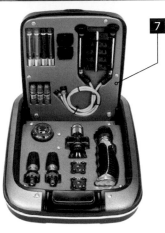

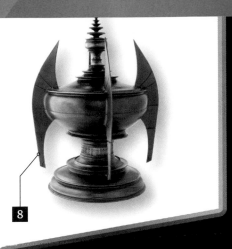

## KEY

**1. Lightsaber**—For use during duels.

**2. Vader's Function Control Belt**— Regulates life-supporting armor and mask.

**3. Holocron**—Stores ancient Sith data, accessed only through use of the Force.

**4. Statue of Braata**—Ancient Dwartii Sage, who encouraged study of the dark side.

**5. Tracer Beacon**—Used for tracking enemies.

**6. Wrist Link**—For remote control of probe droids.

**7. Medical Kit**—Contains life-saving potions and equipment.

**8. Sith Chalice**—Holds rare Korribanian incense, used in Sith rituals.

**9. Electrobinoculars**—Comes with target locator for tracking enemies.

**10. Hologram Watch**—For communicating with Sith Masters.

# Count Dooku

When Darth Maul was destroyed, Darth Sidious needed to take on a new apprentice.

Sidious's desire for power was as strong as ever. This time, however, he did not have time to train a young apprentice. His search led him to Count Dooku, who was once a Jedi Master.

Dooku had been a brave and respected member of the Jedi, and had even trained Qui-Gon Jinn as a Padawan. However, he grew frustrated with the limitations of the Jedi Order.

Senator Palpatine had sensed Dooku's negative feelings toward the Jedi Order for many years and after the death of Darth Maul, he seized the opportunity to convince Dooku to become his new Sith apprentice. It was not difficult. Dooku left,

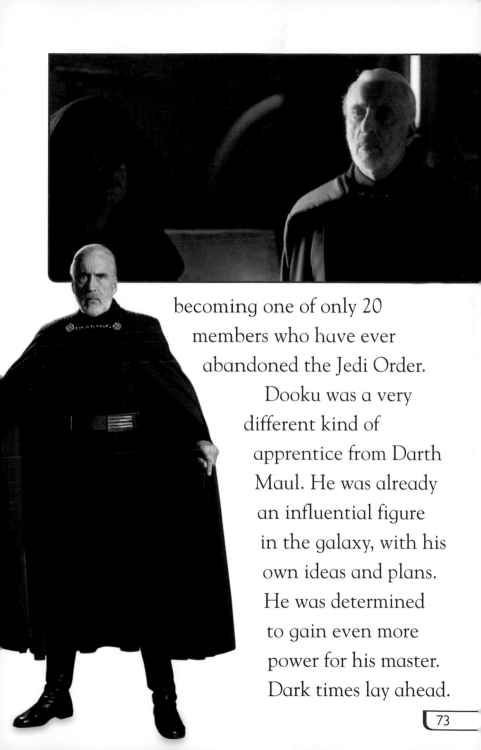

becoming one of only 20 members who have ever abandoned the Jedi Order. Dooku was a very different kind of apprentice from Darth Maul. He was already an influential figure in the galaxy, with his own ideas and plans. He was determined to gain even more power for his master. Dark times lay ahead.

# Darth Tyranus

When Dooku joined Darth Sidious, he took a new Sith name—Darth Tyranus. Tyranus learned how to harness the dark side of the Force from Darth Sidious. Like his Master, Darth Tyranus used Force lightning to deadly effect, and his lightsaber's curved handle allowed him to perform moves that caught even the most experienced Jedi by surprise.

As Sidious's apprentice, Dooku spent many years encouraging planets and business organizations to leave the Republic and form a rival group called the Separatists. He told them that this would make the galaxy a better place.

In reality, he was only doing what Sidious told him to do. Sidious eventually betrayed Dooku and allowed him to be killed by Anakin Skywalker. Sidious knew that the powerful and gifted Anakin would be a more useful Sith apprentice than Dooku, and he felt no loyalty to his ally.

# Droid Army

Before his demise, Count
Dooku persuaded the Separatists
to build powerful droid armies to
help further their cause.

The foot soldiers of these armies were
blaster-wielding battle droids while heavily
armored super battle droids provided backup.

The army included hailfire droids
shaped liked massive wheels, each equipped
with deadly cannon or missile launchers.
These machines could race across flat ground
or shallow lakes, flattening anything in
their path.

Circular droid machines called droidekas were deployed on special missions alongside spider droids equipped with heat-seeking missiles.

Heavily armed droid ships were used for space battles. They included vulture droids, which could also walk along the ground, and tri-fighters. The deadly droid tri-fighters sought out and hunted down enemy spaceships, training their deadly nose cannons on their prey.

Swarms of tiny buzz droids would swoop in and attach themselves to enemy ships. Although they were small, their cutting arms could still inflict serious damage.

# THE SITH DROID
# FACT FILE

The Sith stay away from the battlefield, preferring to send their droids to do their fighting for them. Many of their war machines can fight independently on land and in space.

## TRI-FIGHTER
**Manufacturer:** Colla Designs and Phlac-Arphocc Automata Industries
**Length:** 5.4 m (18 ft)
**Width:** 3.45 m (11 ft)
**Type:** Droid starfighter
**Weapon:** Laser cannons and buzz droids

Nose laser cannon

Laser cannon

Reinforced armor

## SUPER BATTLE DROID
**Manufacturer:** Baktoid
**Height:** 1.91 m (6 ft 3 in)
**Type:** Battle droid
**Weapon:** Built-in wrist blaster; optional rocket launcher

## BUZZ DROID
**Manufacturer:** Colicoid Creation Nest
**Diameter:** 0.25 m (9 in) sphere mode
**Type:** Sabotage droid
**Weapon:** Drill head, plasma torch, pincer arm, circular saw

Armor piercing drill

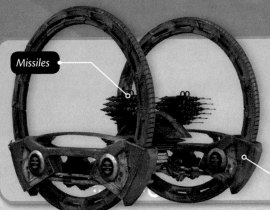

**HAILFIRE DROID**
**Manufacturer:** Haor Chall Engineering
**Height:** 6.8 m (22 ft)
**Type:** Wheeled droid
**Weapon:** Missile launchers

Missiles

Drive unit

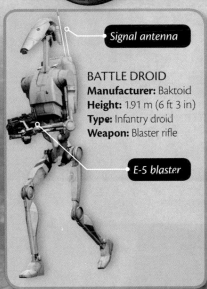

Signal antenna

**BATTLE DROID**
**Manufacturer:** Baktoid
**Height:** 1.91 m (6 ft 3 in)
**Type:** Infantry droid
**Weapon:** Blaster rifle

E-5 blaster

Duranium claws

**CRAB DROID**
**Manufacturer:** Techno Union
**Height:** 1.49 m (5 ft)
**Width:** 6 m (over 19 ft)
**Type:** Walker
**Weapon:** Twin blasters

**TANK DROID**
**Manufacturer:** Corporate Alliance
**Height:** 6.2 m (20 ft)
**Length:** 11 m (36 ft)
**Type:** Tracker
**Weapon:** Laser cannons

Fuel tanks

Outrigger tread

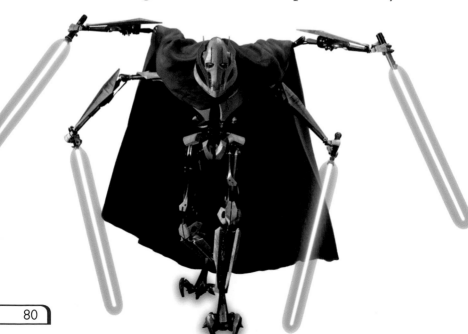

# General Grievous

Many brutal fiends cooperated with the Sith Lords in their evildoing. One such recruit was General Grievous, a warlord who became the Supreme Commander of the Separatist droid armies.

Grievous's battle-scarred body had been almost entirely rebuilt with cyborg parts. The only remaining parts of Grievous's original body were his reptile-like eyes and his inner organs, which were protected by

armor. Although he was more machine than
man, Grievous destroyed anyone who dared
to call him a droid.

Grievous could not use the Force like the
Sith and the Jedi, but few people could use a
lightsaber with more deadly effect. In battle
he could split his two arms into four, each of
which could wield a lightsaber. Grievous had
a long-standing grudge against the Jedi and
took the weapons of any Jedi he killed. He
and his droid bodyguards also used deadly
energy staffs, which delivered fatal electric
shocks to his opponents.

# GRIEVOUS'S
# WHEEL BIKE

General Grievous's reputation as a merciless military leader was reinforced by his fleet of machines and vehicles, designed to destroy his enemies.

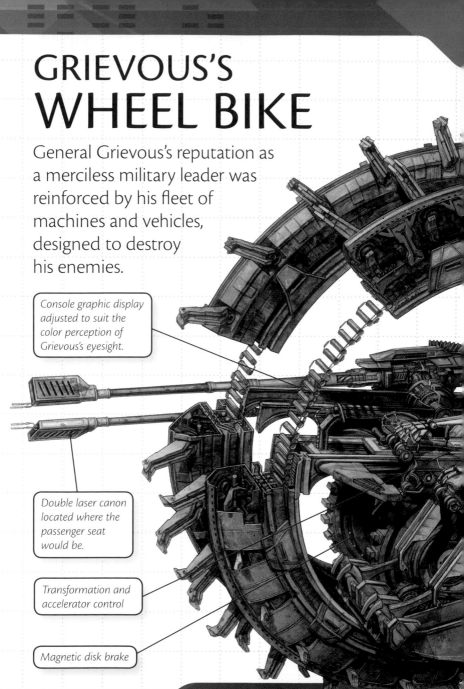

Console graphic display adjusted to suit the color perception of Grievous's eyesight.

Double laser canon located where the passenger seat would be.

Transformation and accelerator control

Magnetic disk brake

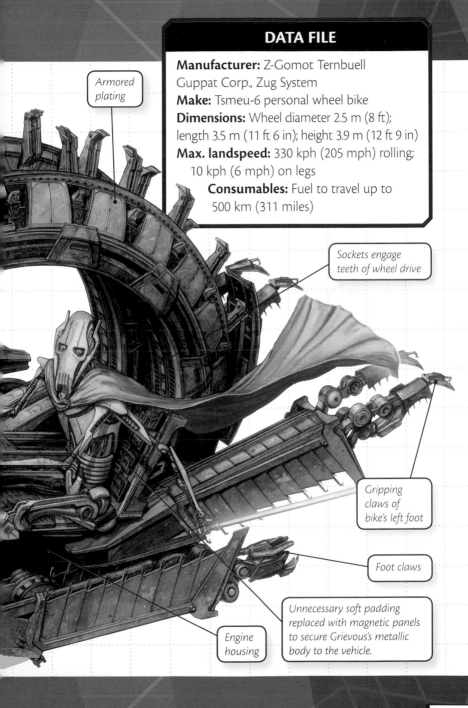

Armored plating

## DATA FILE

**Manufacturer:** Z-Gomot Ternbuell
Guppat Corp., Zug System
**Make:** Tsmeu-6 personal wheel bike
**Dimensions:** Wheel diameter 2.5 m (8 ft);
length 3.5 m (11 ft 6 in); height 3.9 m (12 ft 9 in)
**Max. landspeed:** 330 kph (205 mph) rolling;
10 kph (6 mph) on legs
**Consumables:** Fuel to travel up to
500 km (311 miles)

Sockets engage
teeth of wheel drive

Gripping
claws of
bike's left foot

Foot claws

Unnecessary soft padding
replaced with magnetic panels
to secure Grievous's metallic
body to the vehicle.

Engine
housing

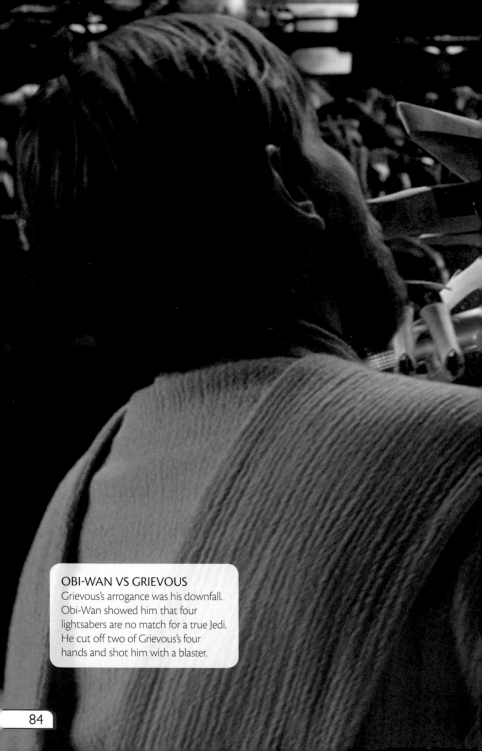

## OBI-WAN VS GRIEVOUS

Grievous's arrogance was his downfall. Obi-Wan showed him that four lightsabers are no match for a true Jedi. He cut off two of Grievous's four hands and shot him with a blaster.

# Clone Troopers

With the droid army in place, Sidious was ready to start a war between the Republic and the Separatists. But he didn't actually want either side to win it. He wanted the war to go on just long enough for him to bring the Sith to power.

Darth Sidious made sure that the Republic had an army of its own, so that each side was evenly matched. The Republic army consisted of well-trained clone troopers. Each was an identical copy of a soldier named Jango Fett.

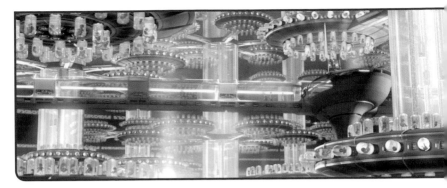

Clones were grown in a factory and trained for combat from birth. For many battles, the clone troopers fought on the side of the Republic. The Jedi did not know that the clone troopers were in fact programmed to be loyal to Sidious. When they received a special signal called Order 66 they turned on their Jedi Masters!

# >ORDER 66

Order 66 was a military instruction issued
by Darth Sidious that ordered clones everywhere,
led by their commanders, to destroy all Jedi.

### LOCATION: FELUCIA
Commander Bly and 327th Star
Corps targeted Jedi Aayla Secura.
Jedi confirmed dead.

### LOCATION: UTAPAU
Commander Cody ordered AT-TE
clone pilot to fire on Obi-Wan
Kenobi. Jedi escaped. Order issued
to shoot on sight.

### LOCATION: SALEUCAMI
Commander Neyo and CT-3423
fired on Stass Allie. Jedi
confirmed dead.

### LOCATION: MYGEETO

Ki-Adi-Mund attacked by Galactic Marines led by Commander Bacara. Jedi confirmed dead.

### LOCATION: CATO NEIMOIDIA

Plo Koon's Delta-7 starfighter shot down by Captain Jag. Pilot confirmed dead.

### KASHYYYK

41st Elite Corps trooper and Commander Gree approached Yoda. Yoda fled. Order issued to shoot on sight.

# YODA VS.
# DARTH SIDIOUS

As the battle rages, Yoda makes the brave decision to confront his enemy in a deadly duel. The dark and the light side clash as two of the greatest Masters of the Force are pitted against each other.

**1** Facing the Sith Lord, Yoda is proof that strength has nothing to do with size.

**2** Eager to destroy Yoda, Sidious fought him with passion and fury.

**3** Yoda matched Sidious's vicious blows with calm, measured skill.

**4** Sidious used the Force to throw bolts of deadly lightning from his hands.

**5** Yoda absorbed Sidious's lightning strike and deflected it back at him.

**6** Yoda realized he couldn't win this time so he escaped through a ventilation shaft.

# Stormtroopers

With almost all of the Jedi destroyed, the war was finally over. Darth Sidious combined the surviving members of the Republic and Separatists under his supreme authority as Emperor Palpatine, ruling over the entire galaxy. The clone soldiers became his personal Imperial army and they were renamed stormtroopers. Many millions of human males were forced to join their ranks. New recruits

were trained to be foot soldiers or more
specialized troops, such as pilots or scouts, in
newly formed military academies across the
galaxy. The stormtroopers were brainwashed
to be totally loyal to the Empire. They could
not be bribed or persuaded into betraying the
Emperor. People everywhere learned to fear
the sinister white-armored troops.

# Empire and Rebels

Darth Sidious's rule was the start of a dark age in the galaxy. As Emperor Palpatine, Sidious used his massive armies to terrify the galaxy and to stop anyone from rising against him. Nevertheless, a secret opposition was formed, called the Rebel Alliance.

This group aimed to end the rule of the terrible Sith and bring peace and order back to the galaxy. The most famous rebels

were the children of Darth Vader: Luke
Skywalker and Princess Leia. When Anakin
became Vader, he did not know that his wife,
Padmé Amidala, had been pregnant with twins.

The twins were hidden away in separate
places by Yoda, so that their father would
not find out about them. Leia was raised as a
princess on planet Alderaan. Luke grew up
on Tatooine. The siblings found each other only
many years later. Like his father, Luke
was strong with the Force and he became a
powerful Jedi.

# SKYWALKER
# FAMILY

This diagram shows the history of the Skywalker line. Character traits from both the willful Anakin and regal Padmé can be seen in their children, Luke and Leia.

*Anakin Skywalker*

*Padmé Amidala*

**SHMI SKYWALKER**
Anakin's mother loved him and encouraged him to follow his own path.

**PADMÉ AND ANAKIN**
Torn between love and duty, Anakin and Padmé married in secret. But while Padmé was pregnant, Anakin fell to the dark side and became Darth Vader. Padmé was brokenhearted. She died after giving birth to Leia and Luke.

### ORGANA FAMILY
Leia was adopted by Senator Bail Organa and his wife, Queen Breha of Alderaan, which made Leia a Princess of Alderaan.

*Princess Leia*

### LARS FAMILY
Owen and Beru Lars agreed to care for young Luke Skywalker and raised him as their own. Luke lived with them on the planet Tatooine until he left to train as a Jedi.

*Luke Skywalker*

# LIKE FATHER, LIKE SON

In many ways, Luke Skywalker's life was similar to his father's. Could Luke break the pattern and choose his own future?

## LATECOMER TO THE JEDI ORDER

Nine-year-old Anakin was older than most younglings, but the order saw his potential and decided to train him.

Luke was 22 years old when he began his Jedi training. Yoda believed Luke offered a new hope for the Jedi Order.

## EXCEPTIONALLY STRONG IN THE FORCE

Anakin's Force skills enabled him to pilot his spaceship at incredible speeds. He was one of the galaxy's best pilots.

Luke used his Jedi reflexes to pilot his spaceship. His great skill enabled him to destroy the Empire's superweapon.

## HAUNTED BY VISIONS

Anakin was haunted by nightmares and fears for the people he loved. He grew less able to control these emotions.

Luke's feelings caused him to have dark side visions during his Jedi training.

## DISOBEDIENT

As a Padawan, Anakin ignored many teachings of the order, including the rule that Jedi must not fall in love.

Luke refused to listen to advice. Yoda told him that he should complete his Jedi training, but Luke ignored him.

## SCARRED IN BATTLE

Darth Tyranus severed Anakin's hand in a duel. His injury reminded him of his impatience and inexperience.

Darth Vader cut off Luke's right hand in their first duel. This served as a powerful physical symbol of their similarities.

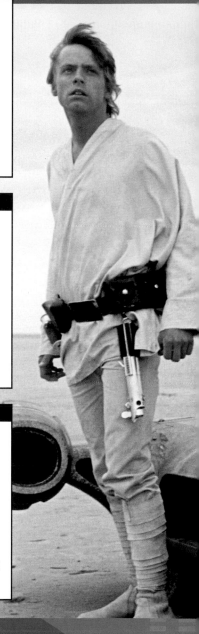

# Rogues and Villains

Under the Empire, crime
was not only commonplace, but
it was also often rewarded. Even
respected planet officials were regularly
forced to do the Emperor's shady business.

When Darth Vader wanted to capture
Luke Skywalker, he threatened to shut down
an entire city if its leader, Lando Calrissian,
did not lure Luke into a trap. However, Vader
broke his promise not to take Leia prisoner,
so Lando decided to join rebels Luke, Leia,
and his old friend Han Solo in their fight
against the Empire.

Even before the Empire took control, there were parts of the galaxy that were wild and lawless. Slavery was also very common. Jedi Master Qui-Gon Jinn met a sharp-witted slave dealer named Watto on Tatooine who owned Anakin Skywalker and his mother, Shmi. Watto loved to gamble, but his bad habit caused him to lose his slave Anakin to the Jedi when he lost a bet against Qui-Gon.

Throughout the history of the galaxy, the Jedi and their allies had to contend with other types of villains, too, including assassins, crime lords, and bounty hunters.

# Jango Fett

Bounty hunters are paid to hunt down criminals and outlaws in the galaxy. The first clone troopers of the Republic army were cloned from the genes of highly skilled bounty hunter Jango Fett. Jango was an orphan, who was raised by a legendary warrior tribe. Jango's unbeatable combat skills attracted the attention of Darth Tyranus who recruited him for the secret clone army project.

On missions, Jango wore full-body protective armor, and a helmet to hide his identity. A jetpack worn on his back allowed Jango Fett to blast up into

the air to attack his opponent from above
or make an escape. His wrist-mounted
flame-thrower was another deadly weapon.

Jango also carried out special missions
for the Sith Lords. He was tasked with
assassinating any public figures that stood
between the Sith and their ultimate goal of
ruling the galaxy. Senator Padmé Amidala
was one such target. Thankfully, Padmé
survived Fett's attempts on her life.
Eventually Jango was killed in a large
battle between the Republic army and
the Separatist droid army.

# Zam Wesell

Jango Fett had many contacts in the criminal underworld. One such contact was the hired assassin Zam Wesell. Zam was an alien whose species had the ability to shapeshift. This meant that she could change the shape of her body to imitate other species. This was useful when Zam needed to blend in with another planet's species without being noticed.

Jango Fett hired Zam to help him carry out the attempted assassination of the politician Senator Padmé Amidala. First, Zam tried to blow up the Senator's spaceship. When that failed, Zam released deadly insects called kouhuns into Padmé's bedroom, but her Jedi protectors Obi-Wan Kenobi and Anakin Skywalker were able to stop the attack in time. Zam managed to escape in her fast, green airspeeder, but the Jedi were soon chasing after her.

The Jedi finally managed to capture Zam in a dark and crowded bar on the capital planet of Coruscant. Just when Zam was about to tell the Jedi who had hired her, however, she was shot by a mysterious figure in the shadows—bounty hunter Jango Fett.

# Boba Fett

When Jango Fett was killed in battle, he left behind a young son named Boba.

Boba was an exact, unaltered clone of his father. He had spent his whole life learning from his father, so when he grew up, he too became a bounty hunter. Boba inherited his father's armor and weapons, including a deadly flame-thrower and powerful rocket dart launchers. Like Jango before him, Boba became the best bounty hunter in the galaxy.

Boba often worked for Darth Vader, tracking down enemies of the Empire. Boba was eventually defeated during a battle with Luke Skywalker and his allies. Boba's jetpack was damaged, which caused it to malfunction. When Han Solo hit it by accident, the jetpack sent the bounty hunter soaring into the air, out of control. Fett finally tumbled to his death in the ravenous jaws of a giant desert creature called the Sarlacc.

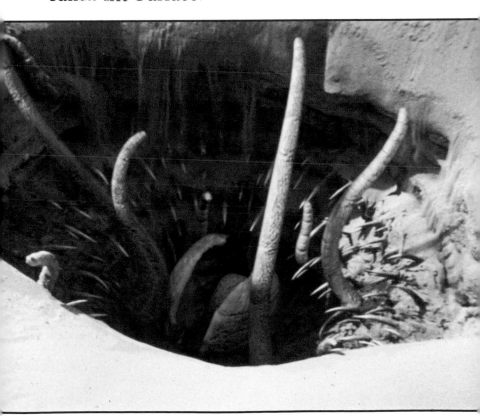

# Jabba the Hutt

Another of Boba Fett's employers was a sluglike creature named Jabba the Hutt. The Hutt species was known for its ruthless ways. The Hutts ran most of the galaxy's crime gangs.

Jabba was the leader of a large crime empire responsible for all kinds of shady business, including murder, theft, and fraud. He lived in a palace on the desert planet Tatooine, which he shared with assorted gangsters, assassins, smugglers, corrupt officials, low-life entertainers, and servants.

Jabba paid Boba Fett to bring him a smuggler who owed him money. That smuggler was Han Solo, who had become friends with Luke Skywalker and Princess Leia. When Han was captured and brought to Jabba, Leia set out to rescue Han with a Wookiee named Chewbacca. However, she was also captured, so it was up to Luke to rescue all his friends. During Luke's rescue mission, Leia was able to wrap a chain around Jabba's neck and defeat him.

## STAR DESTROYER

The Imperial military deployed large warships into space, armed with extremely powerful weapons. But the brave Rebel Alliance's small craft battled against them relentlessly.

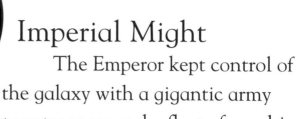

# Imperial Might

The Emperor kept control of
the galaxy with a gigantic army
of stormtroopers and a fleet of warships
that patrolled all the major space routes.
The biggest warship of all was Darth Vader's
personal ship, the *Executor*, which led a fleet
of Star Destroyers. Each of these huge
spaceships was armed with many powerful
weapons, containing enough
firepower to destroy
entire planets.

Swarming around these big ships were countless smaller TIE-fighters, each piloted by an expertly trained fighter pilot.

Land conflicts called for a different Imperial approach. When the Empire discovered the rebels' Echo Base on the ice planet Hoth, it sent in massive walking tanks called AT-ATs. Pilots controlled the tanks from a cockpit in the head of the AT-ATs. These walking machines were thought to be unbeatable until the rebels toppled them during the Battle of Hoth, by wrapping cables around their legs.

Similar, smaller walkers called AT-STs or scout walkers patrolled many other planets including Endor.

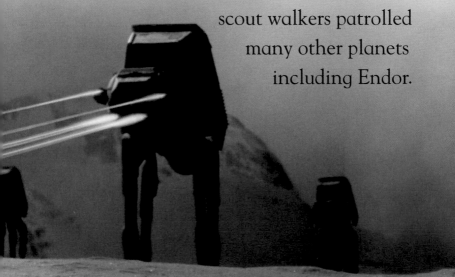

# ECHO BASE
# BLUEPRINT

The rebels had a secret underground base on Hoth, which was the largest base ever constructed. The planet was so remote it was not even shown on standard navigational charts.

01

02

03

## BASE INTERIOR

**01** Airspeeder Bay
**02** Hangar 7
**03** Elevator maintenance level
**04** *Millennium Falcon*
**05** Turbolifts
**06** Barracks
**07** Medical center
**08** Fuel slip
**09** Transports hangar
**10** South entrance control room
**11** Mess Hall
**12** Turbolift cluster
**13** Rec room
**14** Bacta filter
**15** Briefing chamber/ holoprojector room
**16** Intensive-care unit

### ACTION CENTER
Rebel mechanics ensured all X-wing starfighters and T-47 airspeeders were ready for combat or evacuation.

## Ion Cannon

An ion cannon on Hoth's surface protected Echo Base. It could fire ion energy into space to disable any enemy ships orbiting the planet.

# Death Star

The Empire had devastating weapons at its disposal. But the most terrifying of all was the Death Star. The Emperor's superweapon was the size of a small moon, but it was actually a large starship. The Death Star's gigantic superlaser could destroy entire planets. When Princess Leia refused to give the Emperor important information about the Rebel Alliance, he was able to demonstrate the enormous power of the superweapon. With a single blast the Death Star destroyed the planet Alderaan. This was the planet on which Darth Vader's daughter,

Princess Leia, had lived most of her life and Vader knew this would be torture for her to witness.

Yet even the Death Star had a flaw. A skilled rebel pilot—the son of Darth Vader, Luke Skywalker—was able to fire torpedoes into a small exhaust shaft on the Death Star's surface, and a chain reaction of explosions blew up the entire starship.

# EMPEROR'S LAIR

After the rebels destroyed the first Death Star, Emperor Palpatine ordered an even more powerful replacement to be built. The second Death Star's Throne Room was the grim location for the final battle between Darth Sidious, Luke Skywalker, and Darth Vader.

Transparisteel viewports equipped with magnification scanners that provide close-up views of deep-space battles

Trophy presented to Senator Palpatine by Naboo's Theed Council

Receiving area for officials and the Emperor's advisors mirrors Palpatine's private suites in the Imperial Palace on Coruscant

Conference table featuring communication system

Imperial Guards took an oath of silence, making them an intimidating presence

Viewscreen displays scans of the interior and exterior of the entire battle station, as well as tactical schematics, blueprints, and other data

In the style of the Emperor's unadorned robes, his throne is a simple, swivel-mount contour-chair

Deflector-shields power ducts

Darth Sidious blasted bolts of Force lightning at Luke Skywalker

Shield generator

Darth Vader lay injured following a duel with his son. He was still unsure whether he should protect his son from the Emperor's attack or help his Master.

# Rebel Victory

The brave rebels refused to give up the fight against Emperor Palpatine and his Empire of evil. The rebels teamed up with a band of forest-dwelling creatures called Ewoks on planet Endor. The Ewoks did not have sophisticated weaponry or armor, but they used homemade weapons and plenty of courage to overpower the Emperor's well-equipped and well-trained stormtroopers. In doing so they helped the rebel spaceships to launch a full-scale attack on the second Death Star.

Meanwhile, on board the Death Star,
Luke Skywalker battled against the Emperor
and Darth Vader. When Luke refused to turn
to the dark side, the Emperor forced father
and son to fight. In the end, Luke could not
kill Vader. When Sidious tried to kill Luke,
Vader turned against his Sith Master and
threw Sidious to his doom down a deep shaft.

The war against the Sith was over.
Luke proved to be the ultimate Jedi. He
forgave his father and discovered that even
the most evil Sith can still have good inside
them. The light side of the Force was indeed
more powerful than the dark side.

# Quiz

1. Who was Darth Sidious's Sith Master?

2. What was the capital planet of the galaxy?

3. What was Darth Maul's double-ended lightsaber called?

4. Zabrak tattoos symbolize personality, family loyalty, and what else?

5. Which parts of General Grievous were not robotic?

6. What kind of Sith droids attack by attaching themselves to Jedi ships?

7. Over its entire history, how many Jedi have left the Jedi Order?

8. How did Yoda escape after his duel with Darth Sidious?

9. What was the name of Darth Vader's personal warship?

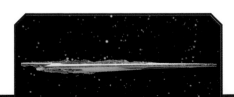

10. Which Sith severed Anakin Skywalker's hand in a duel?

11. The first clone troopers were cloned from which bounty hunter?

12. What was the surname of the Tatooine family who adopted Luke Skywalker?

13. What does the Sith Chalice in Palpatine's office contain?

14. What is the maximum number of Jedi there can be at any one time?

15. How did Darth Vader receive the injuries that made his life-support system necessary?

See page 127 for answers.

# Glossary

**Airspeeder**
A small, fast, flying vehicle piloted by one or two people.

**Assassinate**
To murder an important person, sometimes in return for payment.

**Blaster**
A weapon that fires bolts of particle-beam energy.

**Bounty hunter**
Someone who captures or kills a wanted person in return for payment.

**Chancellor**
The Republic's head of government.

**Clone**
An exact copy of someone or something.

**Clone trooper**
An individual member of the Republic's clone army.

**Clone Wars**
A series of galaxy-wide conflicts in which the Republic used armies of clone soldiers.

**Cyborg**
A being made of both living and robotic parts.

**Droid**
A robot. Droids are built to perform a variety of duties.

**The Empire**
A group of worlds ruled over by an unelected emperor.

**The Force**
A mysterious energy that flows through the galaxy. It has a light side (good) and a dark side (evil).

**Heat-seeking missile**
A missile that homes in on heat-emitting targets such as spaceships.

**Hologram**
A three-dimensional image created by light from a laser.

**Ion cannon**
A weapon that fires ionized particles. It can disable electronic equipment.

**Isolation chamber**
A sealed room in which special conditions exist.

**Jedi**
Beings who use the light side of the Force for the good of everyone in the galaxy.

**Jedi Knight**
A Jedi who has completed their training.

**Lightsaber**
A sword-like weapon with a blade of pure energy.

**Padawan**
A Jedi apprentice being trained by a Jedi Master.

**Rebel Alliance**
A group of people who have united to try to overthrow the Empire.

**The Republic**
A group of worlds governed by an elected Senate.

**Senate**
Elected representatives of all the Republic's planets, who come together to pass laws.

**Separatists**
Those who wish to break away from the Republic.

**Sith apprentice**
A Sith being trained by a Sith Master.

**Sith**
Beings who use the dark side of the Force to gain personal power.

**Speeder bike**
A small, fast land vehicle that carries just one or two people.

**Stormtrooper**
A soldier of the Imperial army.

**Superlaser**
A weapon that combines many laser beams into a single, super-powerful beam.

**Theed power generator**
A facility for making energy from plasma found under Theed, the capital of Naboo.

**TIE Fighter**
An Imperial fighter spacecraft powered by twin ion engines.

**Tusken Raiders**
Desert-dwellers from Tatooine who are very hostile to outsiders.

**Wookiee**
A shaggy, tree-dwelling species from Kashyyyk.

**X-wing starfighters**
Rebel fighter spacecraft with four wings that form an X-shape.

**Youngling**
A child in the first stages of Jedi training.

# Index

Quiz answers
1. Darth Plagueis 2. Coruscant
3. A saberstaff 4. Place of birth
5. Inner organs and eyes
6. Buzz droids 7. 20
8. Through a ventilation shaft
9. The Executor 10. Darth Tyranus 11. Jango Fett
12. Lars 13. Korribanian incense
14. There is no limit.
15. He fell near a lava river.

# Like this book? Try another DK Adventure!

### Horse Club
Emma is so excited—she is going to
horseback-riding camp with her older sister!

### Terrors of the Deep
Marine biologists Dom and Jake take their
deep-sea submersible down into the deepest, darkest
ocean trenches in the world.

### *Star Wars*™: Jedi Battles
Join the Jedi on their epic adventures and exciting
battles. Meet brave Jedi Knights who fight
for justice across the galaxy.